Danger Is My Business:

The World's Deadliest Jobs

by

John DiConsiglio

SCHOLASTIC INC.
New York Toronto London Auckland
Sydney New Delhi Hong Kong

Cover

© Tony Overman/The Olympian/AP Images, background:
© Ken Goldfield/Landov

Credits

p. 4 bl: © Craig Aurness/Photolibrary, br: © Mike Watson/SassyStock/
Fotosearch; p. 5 bl: © Rebecca Reid/Empics/PA Photos/Landov,
br: © Peter Carsten/National Geographic Stock; p. 7: © Martin Meissner/
AP Images; p. 9: © ZUMA Press/Newscom; p. 11 lc: © Stan Liu/
Icon Sports Media, tr: © Daniel Aguilar/Reuters/Corbis, br:
© Filippov Alexei/ITAR-TASS Photo/Corbis; p. 13: © Ken Goldfield/Landov;
p. 17: © Ron L. Brown/SuperStock; p. 19: © Alaska Stock/Masterfile;
p. 21: © Michael Schmeling/Arid Ocean/Fotolia; p. 23: © Klas Stolpe/
AP Images, inset: © Thomas Sbampato/Photolibrary;
p. 25: © Christopher LaMarca/Redux; p. 27: © Government of Chile/Corbis;
p. 29: © Davis Turner/epa/Corbis; p. 31: © Peter Carsten/
National Geographic Stock; p. 33: © Vortex2.org; p. 35: © Stephen Finn/
Shutterstock; p. 37: © Rebecca Reid/Empics/PA Photos/Landov;
p. 39: © Stephen Brashear/AP Images, inset: © MAXA/Landov

Copyright © 2012 by Scholastic Inc.
All rights reserved. Published by Scholastic Inc.
Printed in the U.S.A.

ISBN-13: 978-0-545-34076-2
ISBN-10: 0-545-34076-4
(meets NASTA specifications)

1 2 3 4 5 6 7 8 9 10   113   20 19 18 17 16 15 14 13 12 11

Contents

Introduction

The alarm clock rings. The coffee is brewing. It's the start of another work day. For many people, that means grabbing a briefcase. It means heading to an office.

But for others, it means something different. It means scary cycle stunts. It means live bombs. It means sailing stormy waters. Or, maybe it means dancing. (That's right—dancing!)

Welcome to the world's most dangerous jobs. In this book, you will meet daring people. You will meet people who risk their lives on the job.

Why do they do it? For some, it is a great way to earn money. Others say they do it for the thrills.

Want to learn more? Put on your hard hat. Pack your lunch. Then turn the page. It's time to go to work. It's time to find out about dangerous jobs!

Motocross Riders: *Flying High*

A motorcycle rider starts her engine. The crowd stares. When she feels ready, she speeds forward. She zips up a giant ramp. Suddenly, the rider flips into the air. The crowd gasps.

It's another night of Motocross. This might be the scariest sport on the planet. Motocross events can involve off-road racing. Or, they can involve high-flying stunts. Either way, the sport draws crowds.

Stunt riders ride special bikes. They can leap up to 100 feet in the air. Their stunts make crowds go wild. The stunts can also send riders to the hospital.

Just look at Travis Pastrana. He was the first rider to land a double backflip. When his stunts go well, he wins medals.

A Motocross rider
does a daring stunt.

7

But what happens when they don't? Ouch!

Pastrana has had more than 30 broken bones. He has also had 10 **concussions**. Still, he keeps riding. "It's worth it," he told *The New York Times*. "Motocross is my life."

For many pros, riding is not about the paycheck. It is about the thrill. Most winners take home only $1,000 per event. That's not much for putting your life in danger. Only the biggest stars earn millions.

Dangerous Inside and Out

James "Bubba" Stewart is one such star. He does not do stunts. He races outdoors. He speeds along dirt tracks.

Stewart did his first Motocross race at age four. Now, he races Supercross. It is like Motocross. But it is more dangerous! The tracks are harder to handle.

Stewart earns big bucks. He even had his own reality TV show. But one thing could ruin his career. What's that? Injuries!

Stewart missed the entire 2008 season.

A knee injury kept him out. In 2010, he had a bad crash. He hurt his shoulder. It healed slowly. Stewart got frustrated. In fact, he almost quit his sport.

Practice Doesn't Make Perfect

This sport requires years of practice. Motocross riders work out every day. Bubba Stewart started riding at age three!

Yet, all that training can't keep riders safe. Most riders have **fractured** their wrists and shoulders. They have also hurt their knees.

James "Bubba" Stewart poses on his bike.

Nearly half have had more serious injuries. Sometimes, a rider is killed!

Jeremy Lusk, 24, was a Motocross star. In 2009, he was doing a backflip. Suddenly, he lost control. Lusk crash-landed on his face. He died of head injuries.

Ashlee Sokalski's career was just taking off. During a 2010 race, she did a jump. Sokalski crashed. Her bike landed on top of her. She died a week later.

In spite of these risks, most riders refuse to stop. Travis Pastrana recalls waking up in the hospital. He had failed a 120-foot jump. He had **dislocated** his spine.

"I was **unconscious** for a week," he says. "The first thing I remember was my mom saying, 'Are you sure this is worth it?' There was never a doubt in my mind."

> *Do you think Motocross racing is worth the risk of injury? Why or why not?*

Three Super Stunts

Check out these cool, midair tricks.

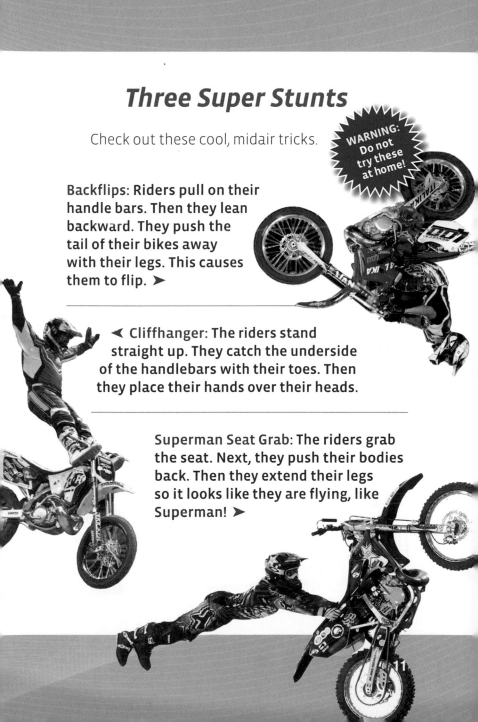

WARNING: Do not try these at home!

Backflips: Riders pull on their handle bars. Then they lean backward. They push the tail of their bikes away with their legs. This causes them to flip. ➤

◄ **Cliffhanger: The riders stand straight up. They catch the underside of the handlebars with their toes. Then they place their hands over their heads.**

Superman Seat Grab: The riders grab the seat. Next, they push their bodies back. Then they extend their legs so it looks like they are flying, like Superman! ➤

The bomb squad's job is not a blast. One false move can mean it's all over!

Bomb-Squad Techs: *Life or Death*

The clock is ticking. A powerful bomb has been left on a train! In seconds, it will blow up. The bomb will rip through the train. It will send scraps of metal flying. If that happens, you are dead!

You are on the Bomb Squad. It is your job to **defuse** the bomb.

A bomb squad is a team of specialists. They protect people from explosive devices. These devices vary in size and power. Some are small pipe bombs. Others are high-tech car bombs.

Luckily, bomb-squad technicians don't defuse huge bombs every day. In fact, most "techs" face mega-threats like this only during training.

This tech wears a protective
suit to check out a car bomb.

Still, a tech's job is very dangerous. "The only thing limiting a bomb maker is the bomber's imagination," says Lt. Mark Torre. Torre is the commander of the New York City Bomb Squad. He talked about his work with a reporter from *The New York Times*.

"The threat always changes," Torre said. "There is always something new. So we always have to be on our toes."

Different Roles

Bomb squads might work for police or fire departments. They might work for the FBI. Or, they might work for the U.S. military. What's in a day's work? That depends on the emergency. One day, a tech might help blow open a door to free hostages. The next day, he or she might check out a strange package left in a lobby.

Only one-third of bomb-squad jobs involve explosives. Still, for a bomb-squad tech, a good day is a day when he or she comes home safe.

"We take safety seriously," says U.S. Army Master Sergeant Paul Carter. He is an instructor at the Hazardous Devices School in Alabama. It is the nation's leading bomb-squad training school. "Everything we know was learned the hard way. That means someone was hurt or killed."

Shhhh!

Bomb squads are like secret clubs. The number of bomb techs is kept secret from the public. But experts believe there are a few thousand. Bomb squads also keep quiet about the methods they use. It's dangerous to talk about what they do. The information might be useful to bomb makers!

New Technology

Over the years, bomb-squad work has changed. In the 1970s, a tech arrived at bomb scenes with just pliers, duct tape, and a safety jacket. Techs had to defuse bombs by hand.

Today, techs try to stay far away from the bomb. New machines—such as X-ray equipment and even robots—have made their job safer. Technology lets techs examine and defuse bombs remotely.

Teamwork and Training

Many techs admit that defusing a bomb is exciting. But looking for thrills won't make you a good bomb-squad tech.

Being good at this job requires years of training. You must work well with a team. The job also requires patience.

A bomb scene is like a puzzle, experts say. Techs might have to examine a possible bomb from a distance. They might not be able to see, touch, or move it. With few clues, the techs must figure out whether it really is a bomb. If it is, the squad must figure out how powerful the bomb is.

What happens if the techs are wrong? Their mistake might mean death for anyone in the area.

"Bomb techs are the best of the best," Carter says. They have to be. If they are wrong, things can blow up in their faces!

Why would a bomb-squad tech have to be patient?

Today, techs use robots to check out possible bombs.

Alaskan Crab Fishers:
Humans vs. the Sea

You are on a boat. Giant waves crash against it. The weather is freezing—20 degrees below zero. And you are soaked to the skin. You must grip a railing. That keeps you from falling into the icy water.

Does that sound scary? It is an average day for an Alaskan crab fisher.

Each year, these fearless fishers set out to sea. Their mission is to catch Alaskan king crabs. These crabs are huge. They weigh up to 24 pounds. That is much heavier than common shore crabs. Most shore crabs weigh less than a pound. King crabs' size makes them popular. They are expensive, too.

The crabs come near Alaska's shore each winter. Finding them isn't hard.

Alaskan crab fishers
sail rough waters.

19

But catching king crabs is tough.

Fishers must travel through Bristol Bay in Alaska. *(See map on page 21.)* This area is a part of the Bering Sea. Here, winds roar at 80 miles per hour. And mighty waves rise 40 feet into the sky. It's not exactly a perfect place to go fishing.

Why It's Worth It

So, why would anyone fish here? Cade Smith says money is the main reason. He is a former crab fisher.

Sometimes, a boat can catch thousands of crabs. "If that happens, crew members can make $50,000 each," says Smith.

That is a lot of money. For some people, it makes this job worth the risks.

Deadly Catch

Hundreds of fishers have drowned on duty. Some were swept into the sea by huge waves. Others drowned after their boats **capsized** in stormy waters.

Keith Colburn is captain of a crabbing boat. It is called *The Wizard.* He says a 35-foot wave nearly capsized the boat. Almost "the entire boat went under water."

Giant waves aren't the only danger. Here is how the crew catches crabs. They lower giant steel pots into the waves. Crabs eat fish. So, the pots are filled with fish to attract crabs. The pots are very heavy. They can weigh 2,000 pounds when full! They hang—and often swing—from heavy pulleys. This is dangerous. Why?

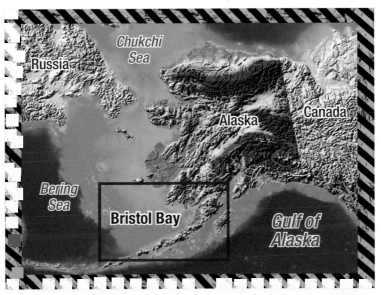

A swinging pot can knock fishers overboard!

And that's not all. The pulleys have huge gears. Many crab fishers get hurt using them. Some get their arms crushed in the gears. Other crab fishers get crushed to death!

These dangers make crab fishing in the Bering Sea a very deadly job. The death rate is 90 times higher than for average American workers. Yet, crab fishers keep sailing into the sea.

"I think anybody who goes to sea finds that there's something that keeps bringing them back," Colburn says. "I can't explain it. I just know I feel comfortable there."

What are some things that make this job so dangerous?

Fishers pull in large pots filled with king crabs (above). Later, they remove the crabs (right).

Cave-ins. Explosions. Toxic gas.
These are daily threats for miners.

Coal Miners:
Deep in the Earth

Randy Cox used to work in a West Virginia coal mine. He spent 18 years on the job. Each morning, he put on his boots and hard hat. Then he went more than 500 feet underground. Today, he hates to think about that job. It gives him nightmares!

Mining is how we remove natural resources from the earth. It is the way we get gold, silver, and coal. Coal is especially important. It is the fastest-growing energy source on Earth. Coal is used to make more than half the electricity for the U.S.

And that is small compared with China. China is the world's leading coal user. More than 70 percent of China's energy comes from coal.

Coal miner Laverne Love checks out a mine. She has been a miner for more than 12 years.

There is plenty of coal in the ground. But someone has to go down and get it. That deadly job falls to coal miners.

Coal miners spend hours underground. They work in pitch-dark caverns. But it's not the darkness that scares them. Mines can collapse. They can fill with poison gas. Miners can get trapped. They can die.

"Bad things can happen fast, without warning," Cox told *USA Today*.

The Good and the Bad

In Kentucky, Pennsylvania, and West Virginia, people have mined coal for generations. "Here, coal mining goes through history," says Cox. "My father did it, and my father's father."

For miners, the job has good points. It is a steady job. It is a way to make money without college or trade school. But it is one of the most dangerous jobs on Earth.

About 50 to 60 people die in U.S. coal mines each year. Most deaths are from cave-ins. Tall, wide beams hold up the walls of the mine. As miners dig for coal, they can move beams by accident. Then, the rock walls can crash down. The whole mine can collapse.

When that happens, miners often die. They can get crushed to death. Or they can be trapped for days.

What happens to trapped miners? Often, their air supply slowly runs out. Sometimes, trapped miners get rescued. But rescue workers rarely reach them in time.

In October 2010, 33 trapped miners were rescued from a mine in Chile.

Other Dangers

Collapses are not the only dangers miners face. Some rock layers in the mines contain a deadly gas. It is called methane. As the miners dig, they may hit one of these layers. This lets the methane leak out.

In addition, many miners develop "black lung" disease. It is a deadly disease. It is caused by years of breathing poison dust and chemicals in the mines.

Randy Cox does not go down into the mines anymore. But he worries about the miners who do. Too often, he turns on the TV and hears about miners trapped underground. On those days, he says, "I wish I'd never gone in the mines."

What are some dangers that coal miners face?

Death Underground

Miners face many risks on the job. Some result in death. Here are just three U.S. mining tragedies.

Upper Big Branch Mine, 2010: A spark from a mantrip—a shuttle that miners use to travel underground—is believed to have caused an explosion in this West Virginia mine. The blast killed 29 of the 31 miners at the site.

Sago Mine, 2006: When this West Virginia mine exploded 18 people were underground. Only 6 survived. Some people believe a lightning strike set off the blast. Others blame the mining company's decision to use cheap supplies.

Monongah Mine, 1907: The worst mining disaster in U.S. history claimed 361 lives. It happened when **ignited** methane gas caused a coal dust explosion. The sole survivor crawled to the surface through a small foxhole.

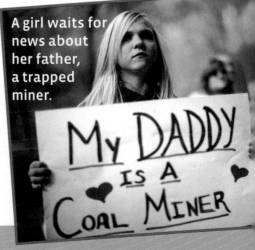

A girl waits for news about her father, a trapped miner.

Storm chasers risk their lives as they race into the path of a tornado.

Storm Chasers: *Tracking Tornadoes*

Lightning flashes. Thunder booms. Most people run indoors.

Storm chasers are not like most people. They do not run from bad weather. They get into their trucks. They race toward the storm! As they drive, hail cracks their windshields. Strong winds nearly blow them off the road. Still, they speed on. What is their goal? They want a good look at a deadly storm—a tornado!

Who Would Do This?!

Each year, many people chase storms. Some are photographers. They seek great shots of the storm. Many more are scientists. More than 100 scientists chase tornadoes across the central United States.

A storm chaser in South Dakota gets ready to study a tornado.

That's where tornadoes most often form.

The scientists arm themselves with high-tech equipment. Then, the scientists risk their lives for knowledge. What is their job? It is to learn as much about tornadoes as possible. The more they know, the better they can help people stay safe.

Terrifying Tornadoes

Tornadoes are Earth's most destructive storms. Swirling winds form funnels. The funnels travel across Earth's surface.

The winds inside the biggest tornadoes are very powerful. They can swirl faster than 300 miles per hour! These winds can uproot trees. They can tear apart homes. They can also kill people. How many? The National Weather Service says tornadoes kill more than 40 people each year.

Predicting Storms

Now, government scientists are working on the biggest tornado-research project of all time. It is a $12 million program called VORTEX2. The scientists are chasing tornadoes. They want to learn to predict where and when the storms will strike. Weather experts can usually warn people 10 to 13 minutes before a tornado hits. But the VORTEX2 team wants to do better. They want to increase that time to 20 to 30 minutes.

The VORTEX2 team is based in Oklahoma. From their headquarters, they can see the signs of a tornado on its way.

This scientist is part of the VORTEX2 team. She is checking out information about a tornado.

What are these signs? They include darkening skies, roaring winds, and the sudden appearance of a wall cloud. That is a low-hanging cloud. Unlike most clouds, it does not contain rain.

The team spots these signs. Then, they jump into their trucks. They race alongside the storm. Soon, they pull up ahead of it. They drop 120-pound yellow discs—called pods—into the tornado's path. The pods take measurements. They measure wind speed. They measure temperature and direction, too.

During the mission, the scientists must be careful. What happens when lightning comes too close? That means the scientists are too close. It is time to get out of there!

Do you think storm chasing is worth the risks? Why or why not?

Five Fast Facts
About Tornadoes

1 Tornadoes occur in many places on Earth. But most occur in the United States. About 800 tornadoes touch down in the U.S. each year.

2 Most tornadoes occur between 3 PM and 7 PM.

3 A tornado funnel can reach 60,000 feet into the air.

4 Some tornadoes are made mostly of windblown dust. Others contain several mini-twisters inside one giant storm.

5 In 1989, a tornado ripped through Bangladesh, a country in southern Asia. This storm killed about 1,300 people. It was the deadliest tornado ever recorded.

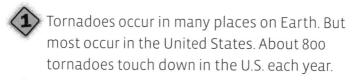

Competitive dancers brave daring lifts, fast spins—and more head-on collisions than a linebacker!

Competitive Ballroom Dancers: *Shall We Dance?*

Donna Shingler has sprained her knees. She has pulled her hamstrings, too. Almost every top athlete suffers minor injuries. But at one event, Shingler had a high-speed **collision**! She went down hard! What happened? She ended up in the hospital. She had a concussion. And she dislocated her jaw. It got knocked out of its socket.

No, Shingler is not a NASCAR driver. She is not a tackle football champ. Her wreck happened on the dance floor!

Donna Shingler is a **competitive** ballroom dancer. She can *salsa, cha cha, foxtrot,* and *rumba** at world-class levels.

* These are types of ballroom dances.

Ballroom dancers can
perform risky moves.

One night, she collided with another dancer. The dancers were doing the foxtrot. But their timing was off. They smashed into each other. Shingler went down!

Quick Step

"It's rough out there," says Alan Shingler. He is Donna's husband. He is her dance partner, too.

"And it will get worse," he goes on. "Dancers are always trying to go faster. If this keeps up, there are going to be a lot more accidents."

Speed is dangerous when doing spins and lifts. Such stunts require perfect form and balance. Going fast makes it hard to focus. It can be hard to do everything right.

Training Too Hard

Mastering these moves takes hard work and practice. That can cause injuries, too. Many dancers overtrain. They practice too much. And they work too hard. As a result, they end up with muscle tears and with sprains.

In 2008, *Dancing with the Stars* pro Derek Hough overdid it. He was just practicing. Yet, he ended up with a neck injury. That caused him to miss a

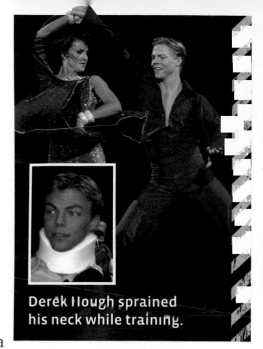

Derek Hough sprained his neck while training.

night of competition. Still, Hough was lucky. His injury could have been more serious. Some dance injuries can take months to heal.

Still, many dancers love their sport despite the dangers. Their desire to compete outweighs the risks. Just ask Donna Shingler. As soon as doctors wired her broken jaw, she was back on the dance floor!

Are you surprised that competitive dancing is a dangerous job? Why or why not?

Glossary

capsized *(verb)* turned over in the water

collision *(noun)* an accident in which two moving objects or people strike each other

competitive *(adjective)* trying hard to be more successful than others

concussions *(noun)* small amount of damages to the brain

defuse *(verb)* to remove a fuse from a bomb to keep it from exploding

dislocated *(adjective)* moved from its normal place

fractured *(adjective)* cracked

ignited *(verb)* started burning

unconscious *(adjective)* unable to respond to things because you are not awake